Building Blocks: Grammar, Punctuation and Handwriting

Year 1 Student Book

Hannah Hirst-Dunton

Published by Pearson Education Limited, 80 Strand, London, WC2R 0RL.
www.pearsonglobalschools.com

Text © Pearson Education Limited 2020
Designed by Pearson Education Limited 2020
Typeset by PDQ Digital Media Solutions Ltd
Project managed by Just Content Ltd
Produced by Just Content Ltd and Danielle Whisker
Edited by Carole Sunderland and Jane Morgan
Original illustrations © Pearson Education Limited 2020
Illustrated by PDQ Digital Media Solutions Ltd
Cover design © Pearson Education Limited 2020

The right of Hannah Hirst-Dunton to be identified as the author of this work has been asserted by her in accordance with the Copyright, Designs and Patents Act 1988.

First published 2020

25
10 9 8 7 6 5 4 3 2

British Library Cataloguing in Publication Data
A catalogue record for this book is available from the British Library

ISBN 978 1 292 37390 4

Copyright notice
All rights reserved. No part of this publication may be reproduced in any form or by any means (including photocopying or storing it in any medium by electronic means and whether or not transiently or incidentally to some other use of this publication) without the written permission of the copyright owner, except in accordance with the provisions of the Copyright, Designs and Patents Act 1988 or under the terms of a licence issued by the Copyright Licensing Agency, 5th Floor, Shackleton House, 4 Battlebridge Lane, London, SE1 2HX (www.cla.co.uk). Applications for the copyright owner's written permission should be addressed to the publisher.

Printed and bound by CPI Group (UK) Ltd, Croydon, CR0 4YY

CONTENTS

Introduction	iv
Unit 1 One-word labels	2
Lesson 1 Understanding nouns as labels	2
Lesson 2 Writing nouns as labels	5
Lesson 3 Recognising actions in images	8
Lesson 4 Writing verbs as labels	11
Lesson 5 Understanding adjectives in labels	14
Lesson 6 Using adjectives in labels	17
Lesson 7 Retrieving information from one-word labels	20
Lesson 8 Adding one-word labels	23
Unit 1 Checkpoints	26
Unit 2 Articles	28
Lesson 1 Understanding 'a' and 'an'	28
Lesson 2 Adding 'a' or 'an'	31
Lesson 3 Understanding 'the'	34
Lesson 4 Adding 'the', 'a' or 'an'	37
Unit 2 Checkpoints	40
Unit 3 Two-word labels	42
Lesson 1 Understanding article-noun labels	42
Lesson 2 Adding article-noun labels	45
Lesson 3 Understanding noun-verb labels	48
Lesson 4 Writing noun-verb labels	51
Lesson 5 Understanding adjective-noun labels	54
Lesson 6 Writing adjective-noun labels	57
Lesson 7 Retrieving information from two-word labels	60
Lesson 8 Adding two-word labels	63
Unit 3 Checkpoints	66
Handwriting practice	68
Glossary	82

Welcome to *Building Blocks*

Learning the rules of Standard English and formal grammar may seem a bit like learning a different language. However, it is very useful – it can help you to express yourself with many different people in many different places.

We hope you will find this Student Book useful as you develop your grammar and punctuation skills. It is divided into units, and each unit is divided into lessons.

The three activities you will find in each lesson focus on practising key skills and building up your understanding. The 'Grammar guides' in each lesson point out the key learning points for you. At the end of each lesson, the checkpoints offer you a quick and easy way to show how confident you feel about the skills you've been taught.

There are three activities in every lesson. Activity 1 is usually very short. Activities 2 and 3 will take longer to complete.

Each 'Grammar guide' clearly highlights the key learning points in the lesson.

Some activities need a simple response, like ticking a box or writing one word. Other activities require you to write phrases, sentences or even paragraphs.

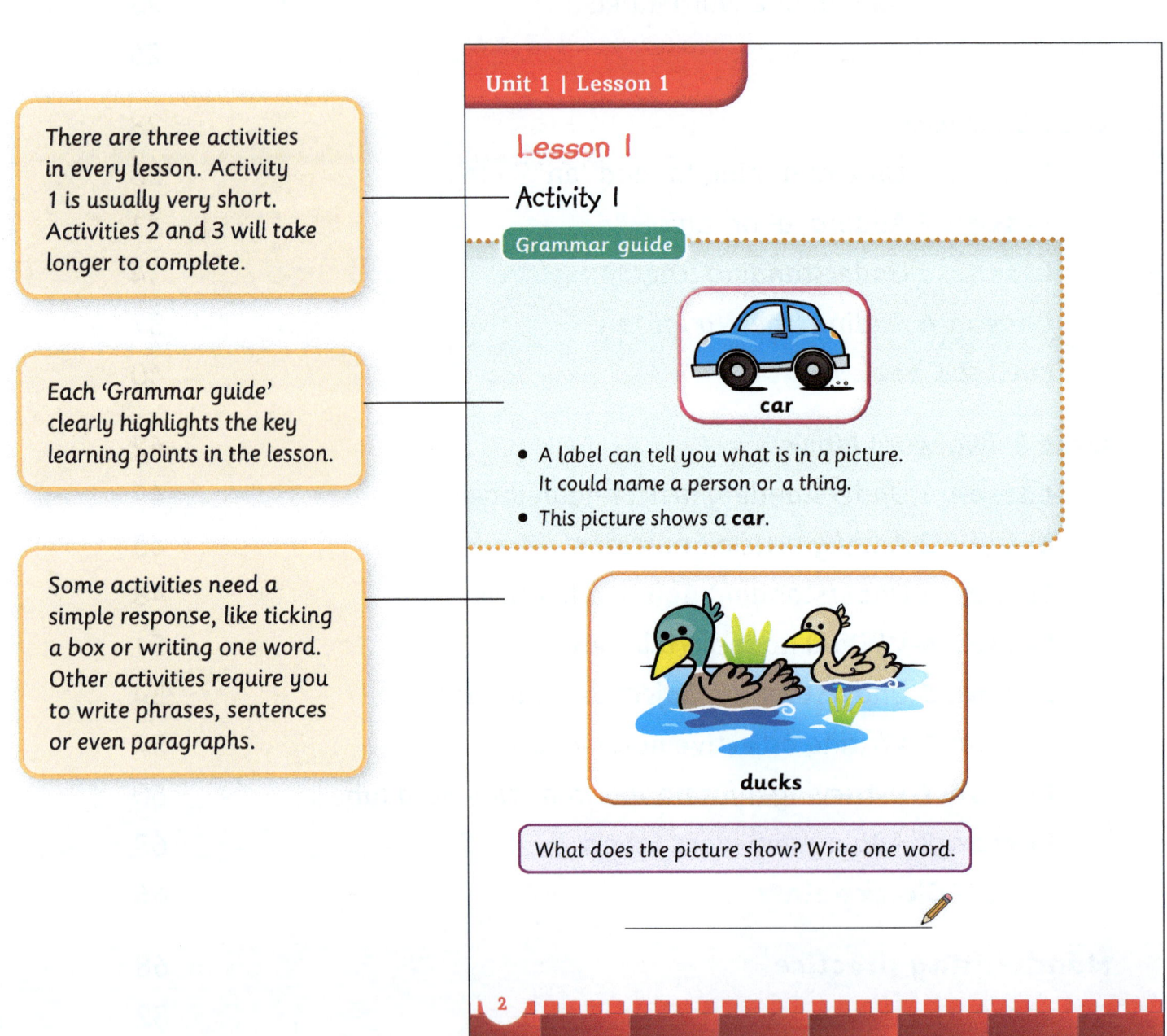

Introduction

Lesson 1	
I can read the word that labels a picture.	☺ ☹
I know that a label can name a person or thing in a picture.	☺ ☹

> Checkpoints at the end of every lesson let you quickly show how well you think you are doing.

Lesson 2	
I can write a word to label a picture.	☺ ☹
I can use a label to name a person or thing in a picture.	☺ ☹

> Remember, you can ask an adult for extra help with things you're finding tricky!

Lesson 3	
I know that a label can name an action in a picture.	☺ ☹

The final section is handwriting practice, designed for you to work through at your own pace. Enjoy practising your handwriting with interesting and exciting activities, and becoming familiar with the English alphabet. With lots of support across all the year groups, soon you will be confident, whatever you need to write!

With you as you learn

> Meet grammar-loving Gon. He's a lot of fun and is always the first into the playground at lunchtime. Gon is determined, however tricky something looks!

> Meet Paz, the punctuation master. She's shy, but she's always more than happy to help a friend in need! Paz always thinks carefully about the choices she makes.

Unit 1 | Lesson 1

Lesson 1

Activity 1

Grammar guide

car

- A label can tell you what is in a picture. It could name a person or a thing.
- This picture shows a **car**.

ducks

What does the picture show? Write one word.

_____

Activity 2

What does each picture show?

book

This picture shows a
_____ .

cats

This picture shows
_____ .

Lin   Bill

This picture shows
_____
and
_____ .

Unit 1 | Lesson 1

Activity 3

What does the picture show?

The picture shows _____, her son _____ and their cat _____.

Lesson 2
Activity 1

Grammar guide
- A label can tell you what is in a picture. It could name a person or a thing.

This is an **apple**.

Write one word to label the picture.

Activity 2

Write one word to label each body part.

Unit 1 | Lesson 2

Activity 3

Read the story.

Kit climbed a **tree**. She could not get down!

Dan saw her. He helped her get down.

Write one word to label each thing, animal and person in the picture.

Unit 1 | Lesson 3

Lesson 3

Activity 1

Grammar guide

run

- A label can tell you what is in a picture. It could name an action.
- This picture shows someone who can **run**.

read

What does the picture show?

The picture shows someone who can _____.

Unit 1 | Lesson 3

Activity 2

What does the picture show?

cook

What can this chef do?

The chef can _____ .

eat

What can Tim do?

Tim can _____ .

throw   **catch**

What can the girls do?

The girls can _____
and _____ a ball.

Activity 3

These events can happen on Sports Day.

run

skip

jump

What can students do on Sports Day?

On Sports Day, students can _____,

_____ and _____.

Lesson 4

Activity 1

Grammar guide

- A label can tell you what is in a picture. It could name an action.

The bird can **fly**.

Write one word to label what the bird can do.

Unit 1 | Lesson 4

Activity 2

Write one of these words to label each picture.

read   write   play   paint

1

2

3

4

Unit 1 | Lesson 4

Activity 3

Read the report.

I have three pet mice. They **run** in the wheel. They **sleep** in the nest. They **eat** a lot!

Write one word to label each picture.

1. _____

2. _____

3. _____

Unit 1 | Lesson 5

Lesson 5

Activity 1

Grammar guide

soft

- A label can tell you what is in a picture. It could describe the person or thing in the picture.
- This picture shows something **soft**.

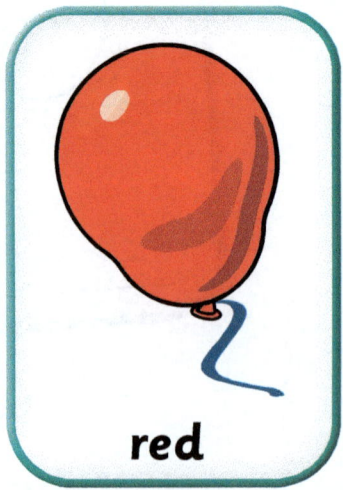
red

What colour is the balloon?

The balloon is _____ .

Unit 1 | Lesson 5

Activity 2

1 Look at the picture. Tick the right sentence.

- The red ball is big. ⬜
- The red ball is small. ⬜

2 Look at the picture. Tick the right sentence.

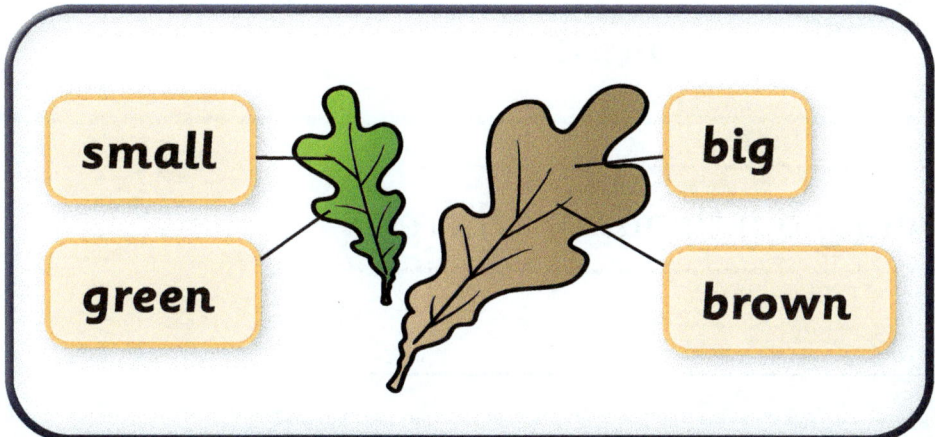

- The big leaf is green. ⬜
- The big leaf is brown. ⬜

Activity 3

Look at the picture.

1. How many big things are there?

   _____

2. How many yellow things are there?

   _____

Lesson 6

Activity 1

Grammar guide

- A label can tell you what is in a picture. It could describe the thing in the picture.

The giraffe is tall. Write one of these words to label the giraffe.

small   tall   blue

Activity 2

Draw a line to label each picture. The first one is done for you.

- green
- fast
- tiny
- large
- round

Unit 1 | Lesson 6

Activity 3

Read the start of the story.

May was helping her mum to paint the wall. The ladder was **tall**. The paint was **red**. The brush was **wide**. What could go wrong?

Write one word to describe each thing and person in the picture.

19

Unit 1 | Lesson 7

Lesson 7

Activity 1

Grammar guide

horse   eat   brown

- A label can tell you what is in a picture. It could name a **person or thing**. It could name an **action**. It could **describe** a person or thing.

- These pictures show a **horse**. The horse can **eat**. The horse is **brown**.

cat   black   drink

Look at the pictures. Circle the answer to each question.

1. What animal is in the pictures?   black   cat   drink

2. What colour is the animal?   black   cat   drink

3. What can the animal do?   black   cat   drink

Activity 2

Look at the picture.

① What is on the table?

There is a _____ on the table.

② What size is the ball?

The ball is _____ .

③ What can the girl do?

The girl can _____ the bear.

Activity 3

Look at the picture.

tiger

big

sleep

1 What animal is in the pictures?

The pictures show a _____ .

2 How big is the animal?

The animal is _____ .

3 What can the animal do?

The animal can _____ .

Lesson 8

Activity 1

> **Grammar guide**
> - A label can tell you what is in a picture. It could name a person, thing or action. It could describe the person or thing in the picture, rather than naming it.

This is a **fish**. It is **little**. It can **swim**.

Look at the pictures.

1. Write one word to label what animal is in the picture.

2. Write one word to label how big the animal is.

3. Write one word to label what the animal can do.

Activity 2

Look at these labels.

rabbit   bird   yellow   grey   run   skip

1. Add one of the labels to show what is in this picture.

2. Add one of the labels to show what the boy in this picture can do.

3. Add one of the labels to describe the colour of this hat.

Activity 3

Amal sees **green** leaves and a bird that can **sing**.

Add these labels to the picture.

Amal   green   sing

Unit 1 Checkpoints

Lesson 1

I can read the word that labels a picture.

I know that a label can name a person or thing in a picture.

Lesson 2

I can write a word to label a picture.

I can use a label to name a person or thing in a picture.

Lesson 3

I know that a label can name an action in a picture.

Lesson 4

I can write a label to name an action in a picture.

Lesson 5

I know that a label can describe a person or thing in a picture.

Unit 1 | Checkpoints

Lesson 6	
I can write a label to describe a person or thing in a picture.	☺ ☹

Lesson 7	
I can tell the difference between labels that name people or things, labels that name actions and labels that describe something.	☺ ☹
I can identify a label that names a person or thing in a picture.	☺ ☹
I can identify a label that names an action in a picture.	☺ ☹
I can identify a label that describes a person or thing in a picture.	☺ ☹

Lesson 8	
I can write labels to name a person or thing in a picture.	☺ ☹
I can write labels to name the action in a picture.	☺ ☹
I can write labels to describe a person or thing in a picture.	☺ ☹
I can identify, choose and write labels for different kinds of information.	☺ ☹

Lesson 1

Activity 1

Grammar guide

I ate **an** apple that I picked from **a** tree.

- The words '**an**' and '**a**' often come before words that name something.

Underline the words 'a', 'an' and 'the' in the sentences below.

1. I am a student.

2. You are an adult.

3. A cat is an animal.

Activity 2

Grammar guide

| an apple | an elephant | an insect |

| an orange | an umbrella | a hat |

- Use 'an' before 'a', 'e', 'i', 'o' or 'u'.
- Use 'a' before any other letter.

Tick the sentences that use 'a' and 'an' in the right way.

1 I have a idea. ☐

I have an idea. ☐

2 I sat on a bench. ☐

I sat on an bench. ☐

Activity 3

Cross out the sentences that use 'a' and 'an' in the **wrong** way.

- There is a shop over there.
- Do you have a answer?
- I wore an coat.
- He ate an egg for breakfast.

Lesson 2

Activity 1

Grammar guide
- The word 'an' is used before 'a', 'e', 'i', 'o' or 'u'.
- The word 'a' is used before any other letter.

Draw a line to add 'a' or 'an' before each word.

a	animal
an	pen
a	cat
an	orange

Activity 2

Add 'a' or 'an' before each word.

1. _____ house

2. _____ elephant

3. _____ octopus

4. _____ cup

5. _____ umbrella

6. _____ table

Activity 3

Add two words to finish each sentence.
One of the words should be 'a' or 'an'.

1. ant — This is _____.
2. book — This is _____.
3. car — This is _____.
4. apple — This is _____.

Lesson 3

Activity 1

> **Grammar guide**
>
> I ate **the** apple that I picked from **the** tree.
> - Like 'an' and 'a', the word '**the**' often comes before a word that names something.

Underline the words 'a', 'an' and 'the' in the sentences below.

1. The teacher asked a student to help her.

2. An aeroplane flew over the field.

3. The book is on the shelf.

Activity 2

> **Grammar guide**
>
> Mum chopped **a** carrot and then she chopped **an** onion.
>
> Mum chopped **the** carrot and then she chopped **the** onion.
>
> - Use '**a**' or '**an**' when you talk about **any** thing (for example, any carrot).
> - Use '**the**' when you talk about a **particular** thing (for example, the only carrot).

1 Read this sentence.

I picked up the ball.

Tick the true fact.

- There was only one ball. ☐
- There was more than one ball. ☐

2 Read this sentence.

Ani chose a blue hat.

Tick the true fact.

- There was only one hat. ☐
- There was more than one hat. ☐

Activity 3

> Tick the sentences that use 'the' in the right way.

- It takes only the minute. ☐
- The teacher of my class came in. ☐
- Vipin showed me the right way home. ☐
- Joan is the friend of mine. ☐

Lesson 4

Activity 1

Grammar guide

- Use 'a' or 'an' when you talk about **any** thing of that type.
- Use 'the' when you talk about a **particular** thing.

Underline 'a' or 'the' to show which word to use.

1. Flo caught **a / the** only train that left at 5 o'clock.

2. Jan took down **a / the** toy from his shelf of toys.

Unit 2 | Lesson 4

Activity 2

1 Isak sees a bowl full of apples. He would like one apple.

Add 'a', 'an' or 'the' to complete the sentence.

Isak would like _____ apple.

2 Emma's mum sees that Emma has left her plate on the table.

Add 'a', 'an' or 'the' to complete the sentence.

Emma's mum sees _____ plate.

3 Todd looks at the snowflakes falling from the sky.

Add 'a', 'an' or 'the' to complete the sentence.

Todd tries to catch _____ snowflake.

Activity 3

Add 'a', 'an' or 'the' to complete the sentence.

1. Can you tell me _____ time?

2. I saw _____ leaf falling from the tree.

3. I have never seen _____ elephant before.

Unit 2 Checkpoints

Lesson 1	
I can identify the words 'a' and 'an'.	☺ ☹
I know that a space is used between 'a' or 'an' and the next word.	☺ ☹
I know when 'an' should be used instead of 'a'.	☺ ☹

Lesson 2	
I can use the words 'a' and 'an' in the right way.	☺ ☹

Lesson 3

I can identify the word 'the'.	😊 ☐ ☹ ☐
I know when 'the' should be used instead of 'a' or 'an'.	😊 ☐ ☹ ☐

Lesson 4

I can use the word 'the' in the right way.	😊 ☐ ☹ ☐

Lesson 1

Activity 1

Grammar guide

- A label can tell you what is in a picture. It could name a person or a thing. This picture shows an apple and a banana on the table.
- The words 'an', 'a' and 'the' often come before words that name something.

1 How many words are on this label?

There are _____ words on the label.

② Underline 'the', 'a' and 'an' on these labels.

a book   an apple   the balloon

Activity 2

What does each picture show? Write two words to complete each sentence.

the tree

This picture shows _____.

a leaf

This picture shows _____.

an acorn

This picture shows _____.

Activity 3

What does the picture show?

The picture shows _____ wearing _____ on _____ .

Unit 3 | Lesson 2

Lesson 2

Activity 1

Grammar guide

- A label can tell you what is in a picture. It could name a person or a thing.
- Use 'the' when you talk about a **particular** thing.
- Use 'an' or 'a' when you talk about **any** thing.
- Use 'an' before 'a', 'e', 'i', 'o' or 'u'. Use 'a' before any other letter.

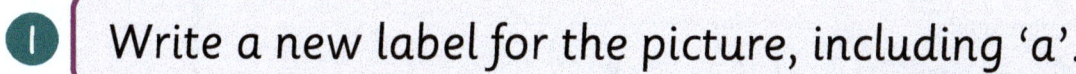 Write a new label for the picture, including 'a'.

flag

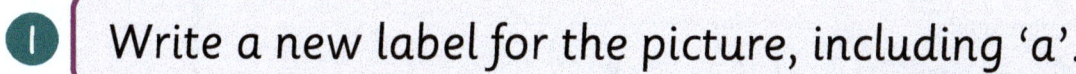 Write a new label for the picture, including 'an'.

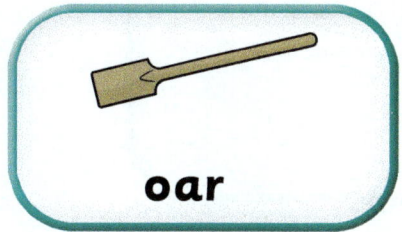
oar

45

3 Write a new label for the picture, including 'the'.

ship

Activity 2

This picture shows **a brush**, **an artist** and **the painting**.

Write two words to label each thing in the picture.

Activity 3

1 The hen laid two eggs.

Write two words to label the picture of this egg, including 'a', 'an' or 'the'.

2 There is one bus that goes to town.

Write two words to label the picture, including 'a', 'an' or 'the'.

3 Kel has three bears.

Write two words to label the picture of this bear, including 'a', 'an' or 'the'.

Unit 3 | Lesson 3

Lesson 3

Activity 1

Grammar guide

Max runs.

- A label can tell you what is in a picture. It could name an **action**, and **what or who is doing the action**.
- This picture shows that Max runs.

Hannah reads.

What does Hannah do? Write one word.

She _____ .

Activity 2

Henri writes.

a. Who does this picture show?

The picture shows _____.

b. What does the person do?

The person _____.

Ann paints.

a. Who does this picture show?

The picture shows _____.

b. What does the person do?

The person _____.

Activity 3

Kat sings. **Kat dances.** **Kat bows.**

What does Kat do? Add three words.

Kat _____, _____

and _____ .

Lesson 4

Activity 1

> **Grammar guide**
> - A label can tell you what is in a picture. It could name an action, and who or what is doing the action.

Baba sleeps.

Write two words to label what Baba does.

Activity 2

> Draw lines to match each label to a picture. The first one is done for you.

Marc cooks.

Children play.

Kit drinks.

Kari paints.

Activity 3

> Add these labels to the pictures.

Snowy runs.   **Snowy sleeps.**   **Snowy eats.**

Lesson 5

Activity 1

Grammar guide

big teddy

- A label can tell you what is in a picture. It could **describe** and **name** the person or thing in the picture.
- This picture shows a big teddy.

tiny ant

What does the picture show? Add two words.

The picture shows a _____ .

Activity 2

orange fish

a. What animal does this picture show?

The picture shows a _____.

b. What colour is the animal?

The animal is _____.

large gift

a. What object does this picture show?

The picture shows a _____.

b. What size is the object?

The object is _____.

Activity 3

Look at this picture.

1. What size is the doll? Write one word.

   The doll is _____.

2. Which object is blue? Write one word.

   The _____ is blue.

Lesson 6

Activity 1

Grammar guide

- A label can tell you what is in a picture. It could describe and name the person or thing in the picture.

This is a huge elephant.

Write two words to label this picture. They should describe and name what is in the picture.

Unit 3 | Lesson 6

Activity 2

Draw a line to label each picture. The first one is done for you.

- red bucket 
- yellow bucket 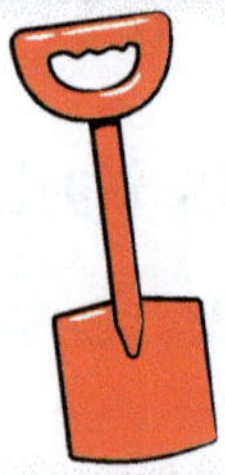
- red balloon 
- red spade 
- yellow spade

Activity 3

Write two words to label each picture.

1 The apple is red.

_____

_____

2 The rabbit is tiny.

_____

_____

Lesson 7

Activity 1

Grammar guide

A label can tell you what is in a picture. A label can be made up of two words.

a horse

red saddle

Ned rides.

- A label could name **a person or a thing**. The word 'an', 'a' or 'the' often comes before a word that names something.
- A label could **describe** the **person or thing** in the picture.
- A label could name **what someone does**, and **who or what** is doing the action.

1. What does Jaya do in the game? Write one word.

Jaya _____.

2 Where is the ball? Write one word.

The ball is _____ in the air.

Activity 2

1 What does Mum do? Write two words.

_____

2 What is Mum painting? Write two words.

Mum is painting _____.

3 What is Mum holding? Write two words.

Mum is holding a _____.

Activity 3

What information is given in each label? Tick the correct boxes.

Kari paints.

Who is in the picture ☐

What the person is doing ☐

How big the person is ☐

small egg

What is in the picture ☐

What the thing is doing ☐

How big the thing is ☐

Lesson 8

Activity 1

> **Grammar guide**
>
> - A label can tell you what is in a picture. A label can be made up of two words.
> - A label could name a person or a thing. The word 'an', 'a' or 'the' often comes before a word that names something.
> - A label could describe and name the person or thing in the picture.
> - A label could name what someone does, and who or what is doing the action.

Which labels could match this picture? Tick three boxes.

big book ☐

Phil runs. ☐

white paper ☐

a pencil ☐

Phil writes. ☐

the horse ☐

Activity 2

Read the story. Write two words to label each picture and tell the story.

1 I have **a cat**.

2 I call it Kit.
I give Kit a **big fish**.

3 What does Kit do with the fish?

Activity 3

Use these facts to label the picture. Write two words for each label.

- Tigers have **black stripes** and **big teeth**.
- **Tigers sleep** in the shade.

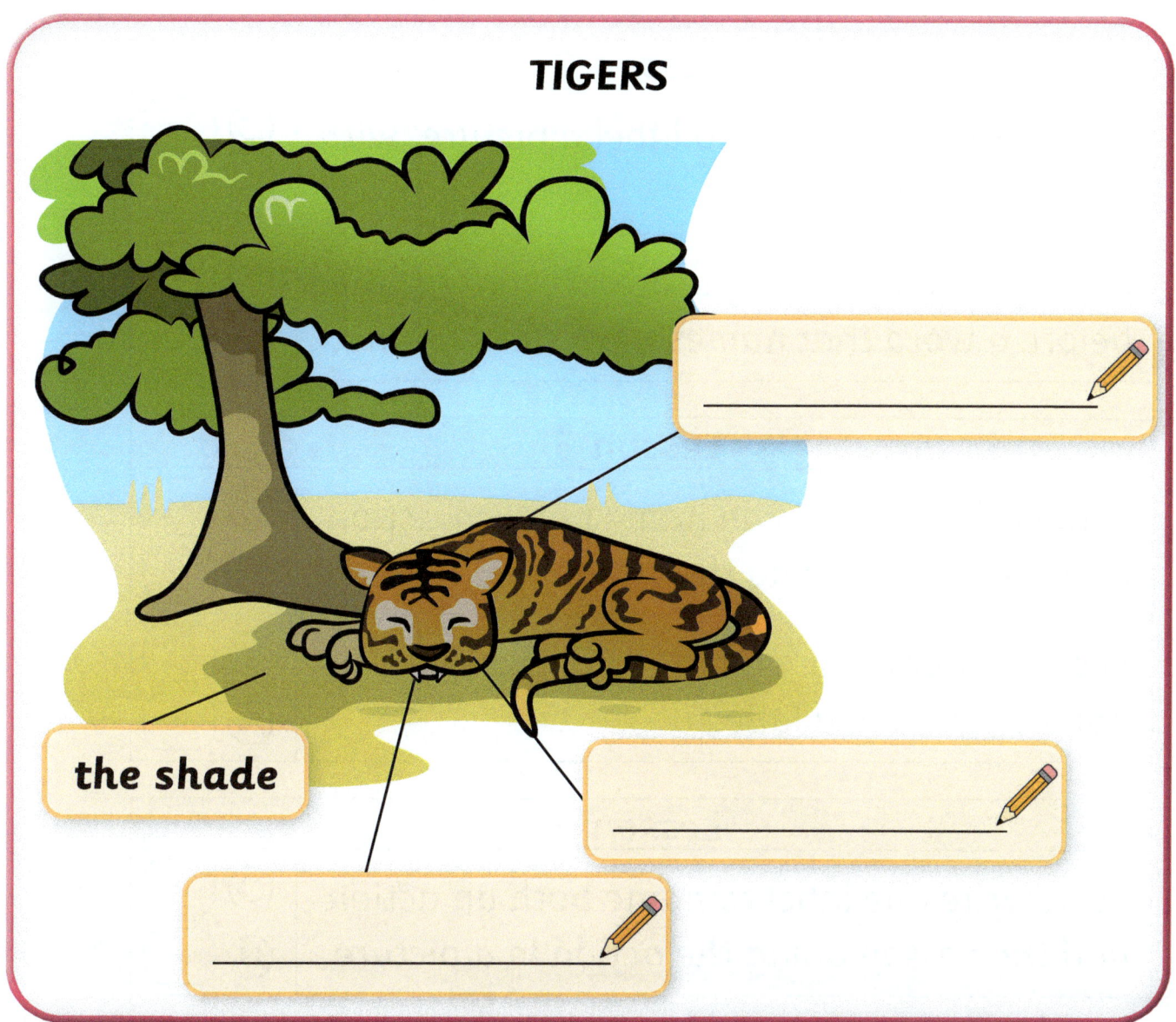

Unit 3 Checkpoints

Lesson 1	
I can tell apart two words in a label.	☺ ☹
I know that a label starting with 'a', 'an' or 'the' can name a person or thing in a picture.	☺ ☹

Lesson 2	
I can write two words to label a picture, with a space between them.	☺ ☹
I can label a picture by using 'a', 'an' or 'the' before a word that names a person or thing.	☺ ☹

Lesson 3	
I know that a label can name both an action and the person doing the action.	☺ ☹
I can tell apart the action word and the naming word in a label.	☺ ☹

Lesson 4	
I can write one label to name both an action and the person doing the action in a picture.	☺ ☹

Lesson 5

I know that a label can both describe and name something in a picture.	☺ ☹
I can tell apart the describing word and the naming word in a label.	☺ ☹

Lesson 6

I can write one label both to describe and to name something in a picture.	☺ ☹

Lesson 7

I can use labels to make sense of a picture.	☺ ☹
I can name the type of information given by different labels.	☺ ☹

Lesson 8

I can write labels to name different things in a picture.	☺ ☹
I can add labels to pictures to tell a simple story.	☺ ☹
I can add labels to pictures to give information to a reader.	☺ ☹

Handwriting

Trace the lines to show the cars moving. Start at the dots.

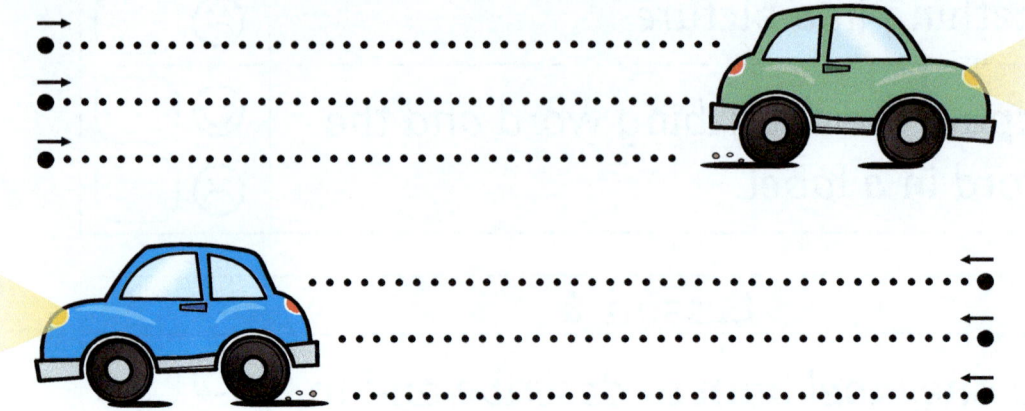

Trace the lines to show the headlights. Start at the dots.

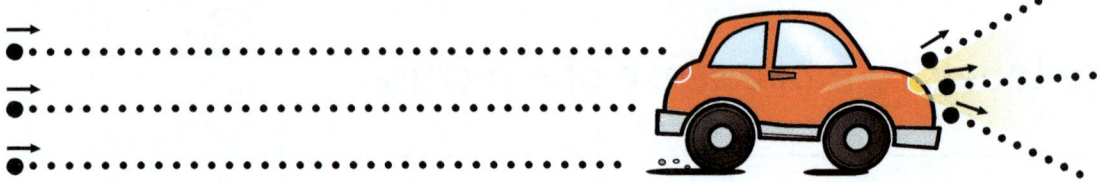

Trace the lines to show the dolphin swim. Start at the dots.

Handwriting | Pencil control

Trace over the balloons. Start at the dots.

Trace the presents. Start at the dots.

Trace the fruit. Start at the dots.

Trace the instruments. Start at the dots.

Trace the lines to start the party! Start at the dots.

Handwriting | Forming letters

> Trace the letters. Start at the dots.

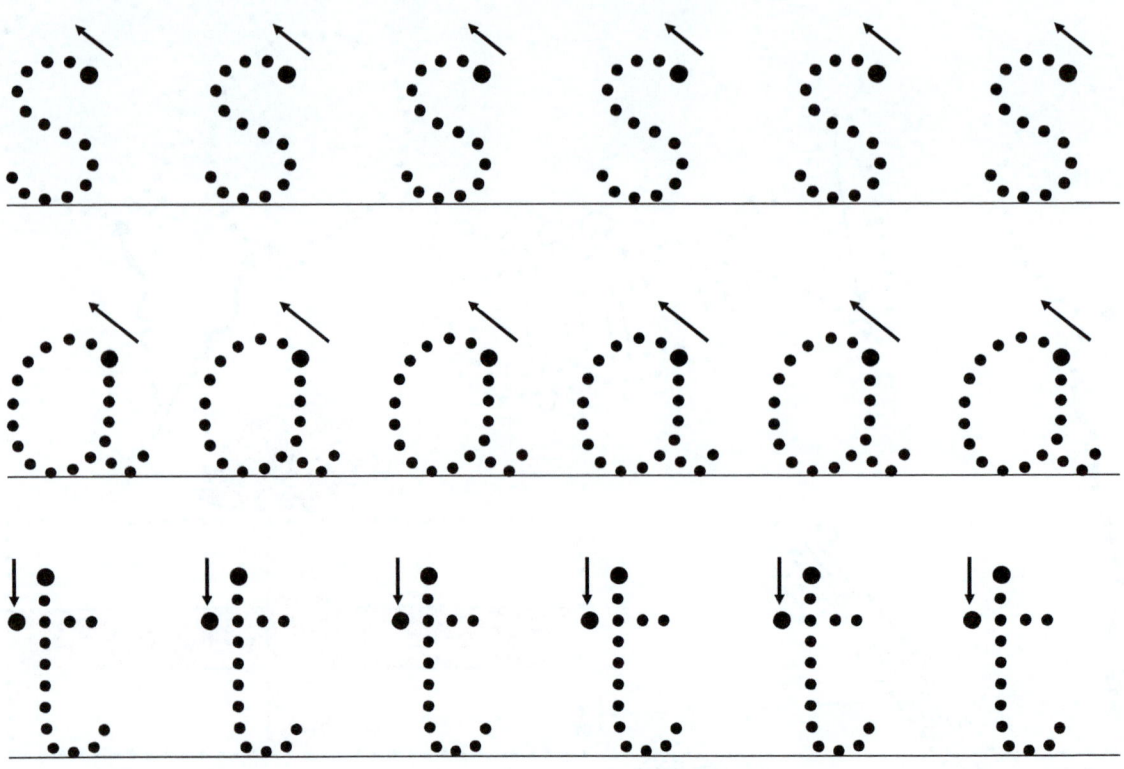

 snail

 cat

 ant

Trace the letters. Start at the dots.

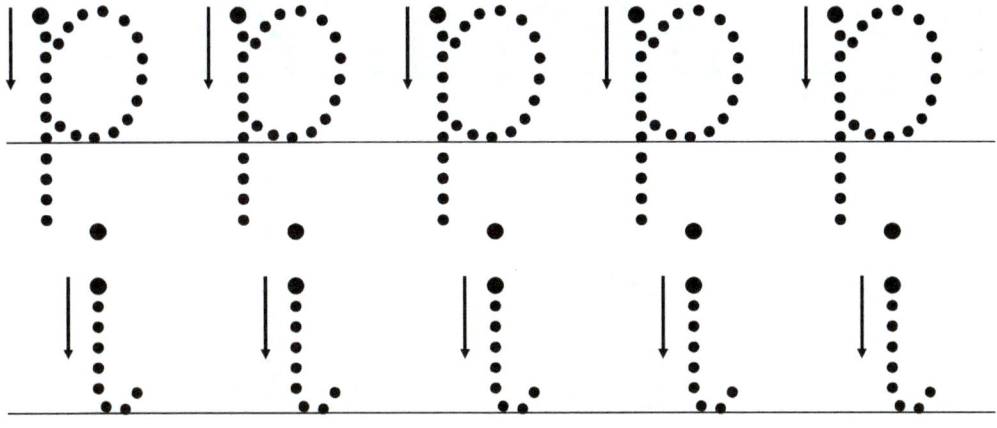

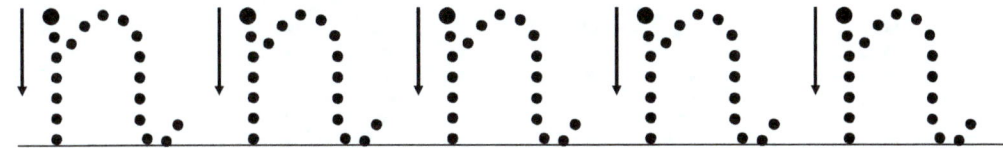

panda

tiger

lion

Handwriting | Forming letters

Trace the letters. Start at the dots.

mouse

duck

goat

Trace the letters. Start at the dots.

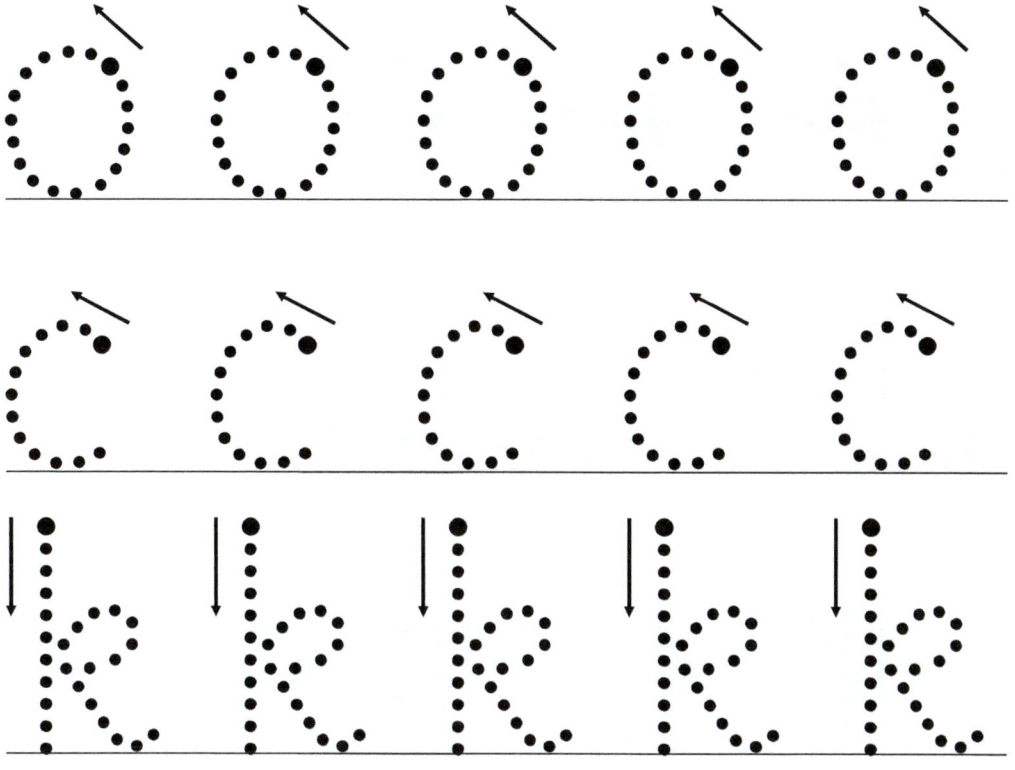

octopus

camel

kangaroo

Handwriting | Forming letters

Trace the letters. Start at the dots.

e e e e e

u u u u u

r r r r r

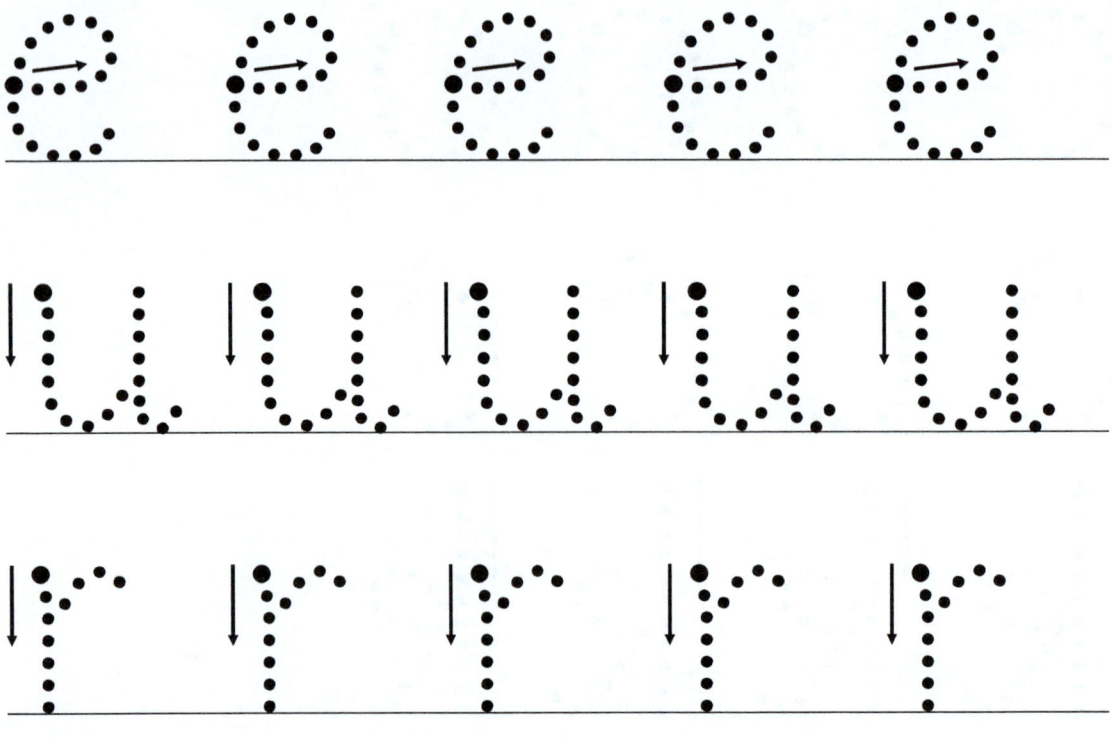
elephant

butterfly

rabbit

Trace the letters. Start at the dots.

horse

badger

frog

Trace the letters. Start at the dots.

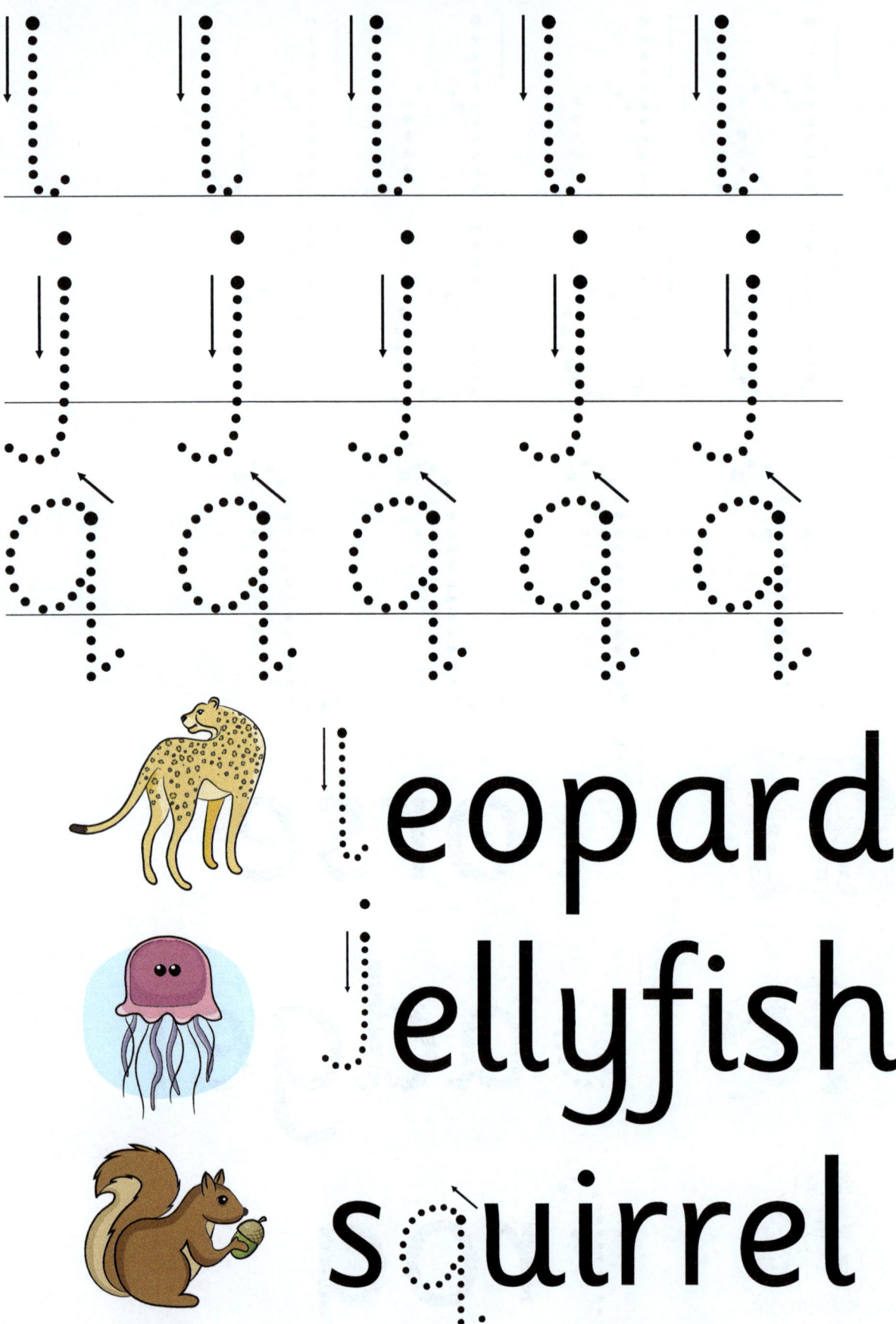

leopard

jellyfish

squirrel

Trace the letters. Start at the dots.

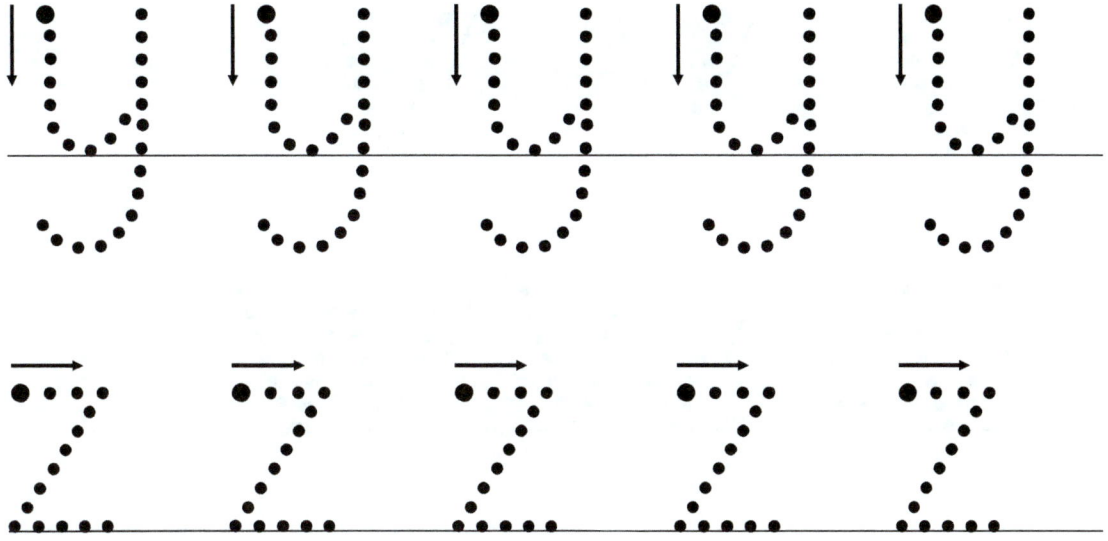

fly

zebra

Trace the letters. Start at the dots.

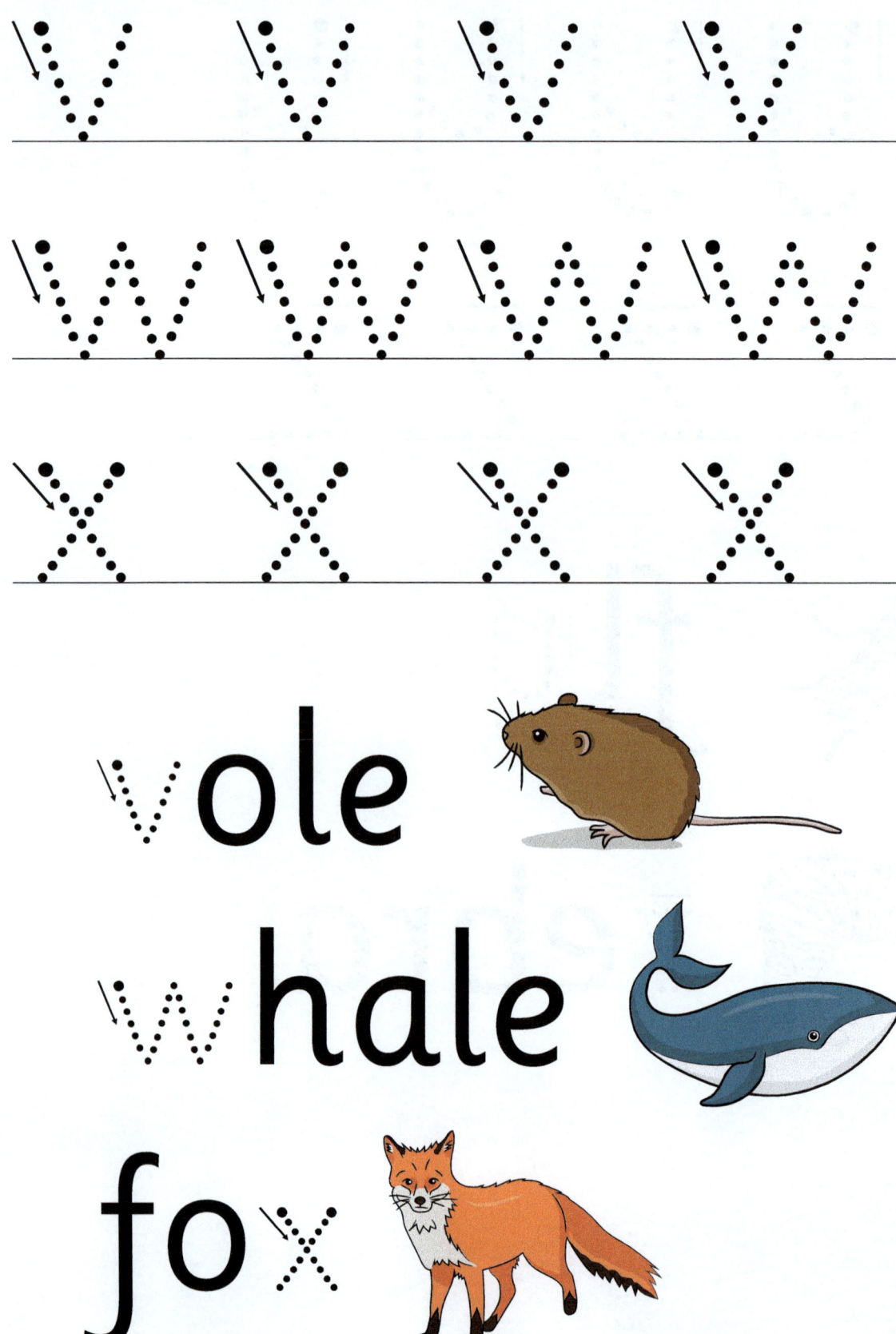

Handwriting | Making words

Trace the lines to make a word. Start at the dots.

81

Glossary

Term	Definition
Adjective	Adjectives tell you more about a noun (for example: 'the red dress').
Alphabet	The alphabet is all the letters in order from A to Z. A list of words in alphabetical order starts with letters that come first in the alphabet (for example: apple, ball, cat).
Capital letter	A capital letter is a larger version of a letter. A capital letter is used at the start of a sentence or a name (for example: A, B, C).
Consonant	A consonant is any letter that is not a vowel. You use your lips, teeth or tongue to say these letters out loud.
Full stop	A full stop is a punctuation mark (.) that shows the end of a complete sentence.
Label	A label is a short piece of writing that helps to explain a picture. Sometimes a label is only one or two words.
Meaning	A meaning is the thing or idea that a word, expression or sign represents.
Noun	A noun is a name of a person, place, animal or thing.
Plural	If a noun or pronoun is plural, it names more than one of a thing. Is a verb is plural, it shows that more than one person or thing is doing the action.
Sentence	A sentence is a group of words working together to make sense, including at least one verb. A sentence expresses a whole idea.
Singular	If a noun or pronoun is singular, it names only one thing. If a verb is singular, it shows that one person or thing is doing the action.
Verb	A verb is the word that indicates what is happening in a clause or a sentence. It's the most important word class because, without verbs, nothing could happen in writing.
Vowel	The vowels are the letters A, E, I, O and U. You don't use your lips, teeth or tongue to say these letters out loud.
Word	A word is a unit of language consisting of a group of sounds or letters which are attributed, and can communicate, meaning. In writing, a word has a space on each side of it. In very slow speech, a word has silence on each side of it.